T0171457

I Am Still a Woman

My Journey

Nina-Ann McCurley,
with Jim Kilpatrick

BALBOA.
PRESS

A DIVISION OF HAY HOUSE

Balboa Press books may be ordered through booksellers or by contacting:

Balboa Press
A Division of Hay House
1663 Liberty Drive
Bloomington, IN 47403
www.balboapress.com.au
1-(877) 407-4847

ISBN: 978-1-4525-0790-3 (sc)
ISBN: 978-1-4525-0791-0 (e)

Printed in the United States of America

Balboa Press rev. date: 12/11/2012

This book is dedicated to Tess Lockley, my beloved mum, my best friend, and the bravest woman that I have ever known.

I also dedicate it to my three sons, who have always been there for me. I love you so very much. You will always be the centre of my life.

CONTENTS

PROLOGUE

At twenty-four, I was given eight weeks to live. I was diagnosed with gestational trophoblastic disease.

After intense chemotherapy, I was given a clean bill of health. I had three beautiful sons and a wonderful life.

At forty-three, I was diagnosed with breast cancer, and the surgeon said to have a single mastectomy, as cancer was present in one breast. However, suspecting I had a cancer gene, as my mother and every other firstborn of my mother's family of the past six generations had died of cancer, I decided that I would take the most aggressive life-saving decision: a double mastectomy, hysterectomy, and oophorectomy. As a mother of three boys in their teens, I felt I had no choice.

This is the story of my journey, my love of family, friends, and life. It is my wish that other women will look at breast cancer as an obstacle to life and not a death sentence, and to remember always we are still a woman no matter what!

CHAPTER ONE

Early Life

My mum was born in Cyprus; she was a Greek Cypriote. She came to Australia when she was three years old. Her brother, Michael, was eighteen months younger. They came by boat, and she set foot in Australia at Wollongong. The voyage took months. Later, the family moved to Goulburn, where she met the love of her life: my father, Alan. Mum and Dad eloped and started the most wonderful life together, as they told me (and so did others). It was love at first sight, they said. I am the firstborn of three daughters, and that is how my journey begins.

Once upon a time, in a land far, far away, there lived a little girl filled with dreams and hopes. Growing into a woman with make-up, hairstyles, breasts, high heels. Getting married having babies and living happily ever after . . . Hey, that is the way it should be. Shouldn't it?

Here we go . . . I was born at 9:01 a.m. on January 14, 1965, in Goulburn Base Hospital to Alan and Tess Lockley. I was a breech baby, and my mother was in labour for seventeen hours. I also was the first grandchild in the family.

My dad was an auto electrician and my mum was a secretary at Geissler Motors, a local car dealer. She had Stephanie Powers's hair. I used to touch it all the time—so pretty. My dad was a strong, romantic man. How lucky can a little girl be to come into this world with such loving and caring parents!

Then there was my grandparents. As I was the first grandchild, I was really spoilt. I used to get away with blue murder when they were around. My grandparents were Nicki (my *yia-yia*, which is Greek for grandmother) and Peter (my *bar-pou*, which is Greek for grandfather).

The Greek name Nicki is Nina in English, so that's where my name came from. My grandparents were extremely good to me; I was always getting lollies and anything I wanted. I loved to be with them. They loved for me to sleep over and help them in their family business. This was great for me. My yia-yia is, and was, a great cook, and we love all the trouble she goes to when she cooks. She still brings tradition to our lives with all her lovely food. She loves to see us and the grandkids.

My bar-pou was killed in a tragic accident on Easter when he was seventy-one, fifteen years ago. I will always remember how he was taken from me. He was struck by a truck and crushed to death. Why does it always happen to such loving and caring individuals in this world? Yes, it was an accident, but it turned out that the driver of the truck was actually a school friend of mine. Really a hard time for all.

My other grandparents were Jess and George. To my sadness, he was also killed in a tragic truck accident—when I was seven. I never really have gotten over this. I loved him, and he left me so young. My Nan Jess is still alive, and in a year she will be one hundred. She is a tough one and always has been so. She lived through two world wars and never gets scared of anything. She is a very strong lady. I know now I have the same strength she has. I have only been close to her the last seven years. I have never seen her cry; she has been illness free.

I was named Nina-Ann, and I would have two sisters arriving to the family later. They were named Alana and Belinda. When I was very young, I thought Nina Ant was a great name to call myself, and for years, I carried that nickname. My parents said I was a big baby with a great big smile, always happy and waving to strangers. I was very outgoing as a child right from the start. It was wonderful having parents so in love and caring as mine were.

I was a late walker, taking eighteen months before I got up on my feet and walked around. My father said it was lucky because I was lazy and it was lucky that my legs could hold me up. I was a little fatty. My mother said I loved hats and frilly dresses as a little girl; I was a princess in the making.

My parents took me to our first home, a small flat in Citizen Street. We later moved to a three-bedroom fibro concrete house near the Wollondilly River. I would grow up here until I married and moved away. Our home was a small, white, three-bedroom affair with a large backyard and a brick sunroom in the front. The backyard made for many adventures as a small child, and I did all the normal girlie things, from playing with dolls to making mud pies. My favourite dress, when I was four years old, was a blue one with pom-poms. It was ruined at preschool by a boy pulling off my pom-poms. Goodness, I have never gotten over that. I refuse to wear them! He actually buried my pom-poms in the sand pit. Mum had to come get me. Totally traumatic. Never returned to preschool. I laugh about this now.

My early years were a fairy-tale existence. My family was and is very supportive, always coming first.

I was both active and a little naughty when I was growing up. I was never scared and frequently ran across the road, which would bring a reprimand from my mother (including a smack on my bum for good measure). Of course, when you are the first grandchild, you can get away with a lot; my bar-pou risked his life a few times to save me as well. I was a little angel, but not all the time. That's why Mum had to put me on one of those baby leads.

My best friend, Lucy Peters, and I were born three months apart. We were inseparable as young girls and are to this day friends. We spent a lot of time together, including going to my grandparents' fish-and-chip shop in the early days. We made a game of playing at the shop—clearing tables and having fun. We stayed many times at my grandparents' house. They had a big, scary house, but we always found it to be a fun place. The scariest times were going to the bathroom, because the toilet was outside and there were always spooky and scary things happening when you had to go to the bathroom in the middle of the night.

But even so, I loved my grandparents and the opportunities they gave to me, as well as the love that they had for me.

When I lost one of my grandfathers at seven years old, it had a big impact on me. I found myself surrounded by my family, and everyone was sad. It was an event so horrible in my child's mind, and until today, I have never forgotten it. I didn't want to be sad at that moment. I struggled with his death and tried to find something good in his death. This incident in my early life may be the reason I became so strong about my own life. Seeing my father come home so upset was unbearable.

I had a number of friends living on my street, and we went to school together dressed in our green uniforms. Hey, they were horrible. I still hate green. After school, we played on the street in the afternoon, all kinds of games, and we always had fun. Goulburn is a really cold place nine months of the year, and on the flip side really hot three months. So the games we played had to fit the season. Goulburn is a quiet country town and we had to make our own fun, which we did. I remember fondly.

I took tennis lessons and was a very good ballroom dancer at about age eight. This led me to competition dancing with my partner, Christopher Navybox, age nine. We travelled and danced throughout Australia. My mother had made a very fancy, beautiful ballroom dress. It made me feel very adult. I enjoyed dancing across the ballroom being held tightly by my young partner; life was exciting and fun. We won many trophies and ribbons during the four years we danced together. Chris and I travelled to Melbourne, Queanbeyan, and Sydney to compete in various competitions. We were able to reach gold-medal status. I pulled out as we got the chance to travel to overseas.

However, I became sick of all the travel and commitment and wanted to leave the competitive dancing to pursue sports like hockey and tennis. I wanted to be normal, to leave all commitment to dancing and having to always look perfect.

Family day was always Sunday as my dad worked several jobs so we could enjoy and relax when Sunday came around. We would drive in the countryside and have a picnic somewhere special.

My mother saved all she could for even bigger vacations. She and Dad took my sisters to America one year. I elected to stay at home, as I had just started working and couldn't really afford the time to go, as I might have lost my job.

My mother was a stay-at-home mum until I was twelve. She became a Hallmark Cards representative while my father worked as an automobile electrician during the day and a sign writer at night. He also did screen-printing and foam letter work to bring in extra money.

I got to see the husband side of my father and realized just how big a romantic he was, as he would hold my mother in his arms or kiss her softly as they watched us play. Every Friday night, he would bring my mother flowers and chocolates. We would crawl up beside Mum and help her eat them; it was a big thrill for all of us.

I have always idolized my parents; they were happy and had a great life. Travelled the world together and were very content.

My childhood would begin to change as I began to blossom into a woman far ahead of my classmates, which brought the young men around me.

Good journey!

CHAPTER TWO

Teen Years

I attended Bourke Street School in the lower grades and then went on to Wollondilly Public School before I finally attended Mulwaree High School. It was at Wollondilly that my figure changed and so did my life.

By the time I was fourteen, I looked more like I was eighteen. I was still a child, but suddenly I was in a woman's body—and not just a woman's body, but a very sexy body. I was a size eight with a D cup breast, and weighed less than forty kilograms.

Because of this, I was often in trouble at school. My friend, Ann Arthur, had developed early too, and we would play kiss and run with the boys. We would laugh about how much trouble we would get into during recess. It was all innocent. We were little girls playing little girl games. But with the bodies we had, it sometimes resulted in being caned across our knuckles, which was very painful. Another form of discipline was a pin on a stick, which would slapped against our bottoms. We were in the fourth and fifth grades when this occurred.

Having breasts so early made me curious about my body. In those days, the girls that were flat chested were stuffing tissues into bras to make them look busty. These days, I think they use chicken fillets. Luckily, I never had to worry.

I remember my first bra. It was just the standard no-thrills kind for little girls, but I didn't stay in that style very long as I continued to become more endowed; by thirteen, I needed a women's bra to hold me up as I quickly moved from an A to B cup, and by fifteen, I was wearing a D cup. I was bustier than my friends. I enjoyed what I had, and I even enjoyed the looks from the boys, but I never teased them or my girlfriends. I only wished they would catch up with me soon.

I loved fashion and shoes, which were my passion, and at one time, I wanted to be a collector of shoes. I could wear anything and looked good in it. I still love *shoes!* Oh, and I still collect them.

I remember the fashion crazes of the day, including the boob-tube blouse. It was a tube affair you pulled over your head and adjusted over your boobs. It was usually a knit that clung tightly and accented your bust line. Of course, you added the tight AMCO jeans, usually in a peach colour, and the big hairdos, and I was set to go. However, there were drawbacks, because with my developing bust line, my father became very strict. The more I developed, the stricter he became. He would check what I wore out, and there was always a battle.

Here I was feeling great to have a bust line, and my father was trying to cover it up or "tape it down," so to speak. Dad was very strict about the boys, because he knew they were taking notice of me and what they were thinking. We used to wear our jeans so tight that we would lie on the bed and pull the zipper closed with a coat hanger. How funny was that!

If I came out in shorts to go for a walk, I was stopped and sent to change. When I returned, I might be sent again because my blouse was too revealing or too tight or both. He would rather I wear jeans or a dress but never shorts, as during the hot months we wore "short shorts," and they were very revealing. Shorts were OK in the house but a no-no outside. It was the fashion. This went on until I was eighteen, and then I could do as I wished.

I was still living in a fairy-tale world, but as I grew older, my curiosity grew along with it. We were older teenagers when we started thinking about sex and boys.

There was pressure in my early teen years. Everyone wanted to know how and what sex was. In small country towns, there was always a lot of gossip flying about, and Dad would get upset if he heard anything about me.

I had a great friendship with a several boys when I in my teens, but it was only fun and innocent—little kisses here and there but never anything sexual. My first real boyfriend Wayne May. If he would call, Mum would have a fit.

I know as a mother now why she was so worried. It is hard to be a parent. Hard to keep your kids safe.

I was still living in a fairy-tale world where I wanted nothing bad to happen to me or anyone else, but as I developed, vanity slowly crept into my special world.

The dictionary defines *vanity* as "excessive pride in one's appearance, qualities, abilities, achievements." I really wasn't like that. Yes, I took great pride in my appearance, but not to excess. I knew I had good qualities and abilities, which I could use as I got older. I set my goals and worked to achieve them in the correct way. I had younger sisters who were looking up to me and I needed to set an example, because there were always going to be rules to follow in our lives. Being the eldest is tough. Girls seem harder these days.

I was a never a swimmer—in fact, I didn't learn to swim until I was forty-one—but we as a family did take an annual vacation to Avalon, a beach suburb of Sydney. There we had the best holidays, of course under the watchful eyes of my father and mother. I didn't learn to swim simply because I was afraid of the water. Even by the river near our home I would only stick my feet in the water. But going to Avalon was always a nice holiday for the family and was among my favourites.

After I learned to swim, I became a real sailor, and now I love the water. I have lovely friends through my first sailing: Les, Craigy, and Karen. Boy, we had fun on the high seas.

I met Ian when I was fifteen. We worked together at a music shop. He worked in the back shop as a TV technician, and I worked in the front shop where I sold music and cleaned. We were opposites, but from the word go, I knew we would be together forever . . . Or so I thought.

It was a heady relationship. I really was head over heels in love with him. I loved how he made me feel, and I loved his touch. The warmth of his kisses and his hands as he held me close. We were always together. It was a love affair that I felt would last, and at sixteen, we had sex at his friend's house. He was gentle as he removed my clothes and caressed my body. His hands excited me as we made love. I had never felt as womanly as at that moment with Ian. I liked making love, the feel of him, and the warmth of our passions. He was always gentle when we made love, and I responded to him eagerly. He made me a woman, as I made him a man. It was so wonderful.

Ian and I were really in love. We would find places to be alone, avoiding my parents as lovers do when they have been told they cannot be together. I wanted to be in Ian's arms and be loved by him. Making love when we could and fulfilling our desires. It was wonderful to be lying with him after making love and feeling the warmth of our love, to feel his kisses on my lips, and responding to each and every touch. We knew we were made for each other and we were destined to be married and have children.

We made love many times at the river and in the back seat of the car like all teenagers did at the time (and still do). A drive down by the river often resulted in lovemaking. For that fact, any quietly secluded place could have brought on the passion for loving each other. Those moments and times are set within my mind and all wonderful moments for me.

Ian said when asked about meeting me,

> When I first saw Nina, I was working as an apprentice radio technician, repairing hi-fi and colour TVs. Nina was about to start a part-time job as a shop assistant in a nearby clothing store, but due to a fire, the store was destroyed, leaving her without a job. I thought she should try her luck at the store I was working at by seeing my boss about hiring her.

Fortunately for me, she was hired. I was instantly attracted to her. I had never met anyone before with such a bubbly personality, not to mention her stunning good looks, I was hooked on her almost at once. We hit it off and were soon dating, even though this was much to her parents' disgust.

Her parents forbade me to see her, and her father even threatened to break my legs if I did. However, that just made me more determined to be with Nina, as I was head over heels in love with her at this point. I was so in love with Nina. I wanted to be with her every minute of the day and night.

Nina and I had to meet in secret, and when we were together in public, we could not show our feelings for each other.

However, it wasn't long before the cat was out of the bag, and her parents confronted us. We admitted our love for each other and her parents gave in, allowing us to see each other.

After a lengthy engagement of two years, we got married . . .

Back to me!

I dropped out of school and worked full time at the music shop. I knew what I wanted for my life. I left school, going just four months of my year 11. I really was not into studying at all. I was more into the sports world in school and spent years playing hockey and basketball, as well as enjoying the small country town life, knowing you have to you make it what you want it to be.

There really is not much to do. No beach, only a river. But we played in the cemetery in the moonlight, chasing each other in the dark. My friend, Kerrie O'Connor, lived in a farm across from the cemetery. All our friends lived close by, some on our street so we would play tennis and games after school. I had my dear friend,

Peter, and his sisters, Joan and Debby, who lived next door, and we played all the time. They were fun to be around. It really hurt me when they lost their parents in two separate tragedies in one year.

I was like any other kid when I was growing up when it came to having pets. I had a pet turtle, which I adored. He either got away, was kidnapped, or was stolen—who knows?—but I searched for what seemed like forever and never found him. He never came home, although I don't think he could have found his way anyway.

I also had a dog for twelve years. His name was Benny. He was such a great dog. He got his name when he arrived during a Benny Hill program. I took one look at him, and he became Benny. He was a great friend to me, always tagging along or playing with me in the yard or by the river. Sadly, he was hit in our driveway because an idiot driver tried to avoid hitting a truck and hit Benny instead. Having to let him go hurt us deeply. Dad made the decision after seeing Benny had lost a leg and was in a very bad way, and was so old. Twelve years old. That was a hard time for the family. I thought I would die; dogs are so loved.

We rode pushbikes around town all the time. There was a corner in our town where there was a weir we liked to hang out at. It was called Marsden's Weir. There was a shiny steam train that was really beautiful, and we would spend time just looking at it or touching it. This was also the hangout for the local séances, which were very scary indeed. During a séance, there was a lot of screaming and laughter. We enjoyed the fun. It was harmless, or so we thought, but to tell the truth, I am still scared of ghosts. I wonder if this is the reason why. Of course, here I must mention the haunted house. Oh, every old country town had one. Debbie Cambridge, Ann Arthur, Lesley Burrows, Cheri Gray, and I had some fun times there, or running from there while screaming. Girlfriends are very fun. So was the local park called Belmore Park. That is where we had the odd drink underage.

The music shop was my first job, and then I went to Allen's where I worked on the front desk doing sales, modelling, and accounts. I moved on to work at Veinnaworld a German restaurant and service station. It became famous as the home of Rambo, a local icon.

I later worked at the IMB building society, as a teller and doing promotions. So I have had many jobs. I still have many jobs. My journey continued.

Good journey!

Chapter Three

Leaving Home

I was engaged at nineteen and married when I was twenty-one. Ian is two years older and the middle child of five. He lived on a farm where they raised kangaroos, emus, and many other animals. They would actually run through his house. It was a local spot for tourists. He was the country boy and I was the city girl, so to speak. Ian was a great motorcycle rider and loved to go camping. I didn't mind the motorcycle, not that I liked to get on it, but I wasn't a camper by any means. Camping to me is when room service is late. I love sleeping under the stars—that is, five stars.

On January 11, 1986, we were married at a lovely heritage church in Goulburn. The day was a typical January day: stinking hot. We had three bridesmaids and three groomsmen, so it was a big do for everyone concerned.

My dress was really very pretty and full. It had a great big hoop petticoat, was white with sequins, and had big bell sleeves. Don't laugh. This was the fashion back then. I was three days off twenty-one years old. Mum was great, as she and the girls helped me get ready. My dress had been bought in the United States, as were the shoes. They were lace white satin and stunning, and I loved them so much. My jewellery was simple and elegant. I left my hair down and wore a veil.

A woman's wedding day is the most exciting day in her life, and it was just as I had imagined. Magic and fairy tale. The venue was set in white, and it was really amazing. Then we stayed at the hotel at the function centre, but we kept that a secret. I am pretty sure our friends may have had a few surprises up their sleeves, so no one knew. Secrets are fun.

Dad made the wedding even more special by giving me my twenty-first key during the ceremony. My mother and father were amazing. What a lovely wedding it was with one hundred guests.

As with many big weddings, there were problems, including the hire cars were running late; one even broke down. My hair had to be redone as the heat created chaos with it.

Even with the minor miscues, it was a perfect wedding. I wore a fairy-tale dress, the venue was spectacular, and there were family and friends. The original list had been enormous, and we had to cut it down to fit. I think we cut fifty names off. So hard.

The service was at St. Saviors Cathedral, a huge, breathtaking church. My mum and dad had been married there as well, so I was very excited to be there. The service was a nice Church of England ceremony that was simple but lovely. We then had photos taken in the front of the cathedral and proceeded to the reception. When we arrived, we walked down stairs covered with white material and walked through an archway to be greeted by the crowd with applause and whistles.

We ate and later danced before going to our hotel to spend our first night as husband and wife. By the way, Ian hated dancing and I really was amazed he did it. He did not want to. Ian made me feel the loveliest woman in the world that night as we made love and awoke the next morning in each other's arms, a new world awaiting us.

The unhappy part of all the wonderful things that were happening was we would have to leave the country and move to

Sydney, away from my mum and dad and friends and family. It was a really scary time for me.

Sydney is a busy city and it took a lot to make that move. It was hard, but I was excited to begin my life with Ian and to start a family. My dream was becoming a reality, and I thought, *How good is that?*

I had always wanted children. Some of my friends wanted fancy jobs and a place in society, but I wanted children that I could love and care for and watch become men and women with families of their own.

We moved to Marsfield in Sydney. It was nice, small unit, comfortable and just right for a couple beginning their lives together. And it was not like the big city. There were birds and cats and lots of trees, which helped me to feel a little like I was home.

It was far enough from the Sydney, an hour bus ride, that it made me feel like I was back home in Goulburn. When you are in the country, everything is close so it takes five minutes to go here or there. That includes parking the car.

Sydney, however, was a total shock to me. It took from one to one and a half hours to get to work. I had to rise early, shower, put on my make-up, and rush to catch a bus. I hated that. The bus stop was at a corner, near the apartment, which was OK. Since there were no trains, the bus was the only way to get to work. We couldn't drive into Sydney as parking was an issue every day.

I had a few jobs while we were in Marsfield. I worked at the local pharmacy and also for Elizabeth Arden as a travelling make-up artist. This was a really fun, dressy job. I loved the freedom of not being stuck in one place, and one of the perks was free make-up. What a hoot. We even had the opportunity to work fashion shows, which was really fun.

I started out at a menswear store as the buyer of boys apparel. It was tough, and I never really liked it that much. I always seemed to get bored with jobs and loved moving around. Not sure why I love beginning a new job. Maybe it is the challenge and wondering where the job will take me, and once I arrive, I feel like I have to move on.

It was hard moving and living in Sydney after being in the country, so there were some ups and downs in the first three years of marriage. We moved from Sydney to the Central Coast in 1988. This was a hard one. Ian had some exciting stuff going on with a project with Dick Smith, a Solar car race. Ian was pretty excited, as he had built the car and then got to race it. I was proud of him, but then he had to leave for a while. Since I had started a new job in a new place, I decided not to go. I was very excited to see him on the news broadcasts; he was a very smart man. But I found it hard being in a new place. We moved to Narara, which means "black snake" in Aboriginal. I hate snakes. How did that go? It was a horrid place; a few mad things happened on our street, and it was a bit of a rough place to live. We did have some really nice friends on our street though.

Other exciting things happened, but when I found out I was pregnant, I was elated. I had a small body inside my womb—a new life and something I had wanted for so long. This wanted miracle would soon turn into a nightmare, for Ian and I and I would be saddled with something a twenty-four-year-old should never have to face.

Good journey!

CHAPTER FOUR

First Bout with Cancer

The first cancer battle was in 1989, three years into our marriage. When I found out I was pregnant, I was elated. We had been trying to make me pregnant as Ian knew how much I wanted to have a child. He had wanted to get the house first.

At seven weeks pregnant, I started bleeding. I went to bed and the lady doctor told me whatever will be will be. I stayed in bed for three days and the bleeding stopped. I thought it was going to be OK!

Then at nineteen and half weeks, the bleeding started again. They rushed me in for an ultrasound. I saw the baby, and I was happy. But the guy doing the ultrasound was quiet and concerned. I said to him, "I can see it's OK." He said, "Sadly, there is no heart beat. The baby has been dead a little while."

I could not imagine that this was happening to me. My first baby and nearly halfway. "Are you serious?" I thought it was a cruel joke. He said he was not meant to tell me, but the doctor was running late and he didn't want me thinking that everything was OK. I felt like I had been hit by a bus. Numb. Afraid . . . I had to sit and wait with the dead baby to see my doctor. I was so crushed and in major shock. To make the matter worse, there were no beds, so Ian and I went home and had to go to emergency the next day.

What a night, sleeping with my baby dead inside me. *Why?*

I lost a baby girl, the doctors said the placenta had cut off her blood supply and she died. This was such a hard day, you know. My world crashed around me and I was plunged into a dark depression.

My desire to have a child had ended with its death, and as I was trying to adapt to that loss, which is really hard, four weeks later I find myself battling for my own life after being told I had cancer.

I had been diagnosed with a rare form of cancer called choriocarcinoma. Choriocarcinoma is a malignant and aggressive cancer of the placenta. Gestational trophoblastic disease, it is characterized by early haematogenous spreading to other parts. To top that off, at the time they knew very little about it. It had gone everywhere, as I was pregnant. I had twice as much blood so it spread to all my organs. One week of tests in hospital to establish I was in really big trouble.

I was in very bad pain for weeks after losing my baby and learning, at the same time, I had a cancer. I was a young woman full of life, wanting to bring into the world children of her own to care for and love. I was on the brink of losing my own life. I was working in a Pharmacy in Wyoming. There I met my very good friend, Sandra Munro. (We are very close. She is now thirty-nine kilograms and fighting her own battle. She had bowel cancer. She has been so good to me.)

The doctors confirmed I needed chemotherapy, but they were unsure of what would happen and I was told I have eight weeks to live. In my mind, I was screaming, "No! This can't be. I have so much to offer to the world!" I cried and sank deeper into my depression, but somewhere in that depression, I saw a light, something to hold onto and something that pushed me forward to regain the fight that was in me. My mum sobbed. She was with me at the time. We were about to leave to go away when the call came in: "You must come to the doctor immediately."

The chemotherapies began soon after. I experienced the nausea and hair loss, and a growing fear began to fill my mind: a fear of losing my feminine appeal. The first three chemos did not work. Not one of them even made a difference. After the first week of tests, it appeared I had four weeks to live.

Chemo the first the first time was pretty scary, but how things change in time and with research. Once a week, I was admitted for twenty-four hours into the hospital, and by the time I got out, about twenty-seven hours had passed.

When you hear the word *chemo,* it really scares you. They inject you in your arm. It's very invasive and you can feel it. I thought I was having dry ice pumped through my veins; it is not a very nice feeling. It was methotrexate, which is not a really friendly chemo. It's always fresh in my mind how much chemo hurts.

You cannot possibly imagine what it is like. A time bomb ticking in my body, and three weeks in a row, I was told the chemo was not working. My doctors were telling me I only had eight weeks to live and one week to find a path for me with many tests, and now there were the chemo failures one after the other.

I used to lie there and fill my head with happy things, but I would cry and weep. In my mind, I had to be here. I wanted to be a mum. I had to survive to do that. The lady in my room cried all night. She was dying, and to top it off, I was across from the maternity ward so I had to watch all the mums with their babies. This was really hard for me.

One month would soon be gone. Can I tell you I was so afraid, so terrified of dying? In my darkest moments, I wrote a diary filled with the fear and terror. No one can imagine how hard this time was, knowing that the doctors were trying but (it appeared) I wasn't going to make it!

Trust is a scary thing in a cancer battle. I had no idea how to save myself, but I had to trust people, and that appeared to be failing. Many, many tears were shed, and at the same time my mind was starting to pull me to a place so scary, so frightening, I could not bear to even think of a future. I was afraid I was being drawn to a dark place. I knew I had to stay positive, but I was really afraid of dying. I was afraid that my world and my hopes would be crushed forever. I have a happy place I go to. It's called Barbie Land. It's a safe place full of laughter and fun; no bad things happen there. I was trying to stay there but sometimes got dragged to the dark place! (Big hole, no way out!)

I remember waking up one day at 3 a.m. in pain, and I was lying in the darkness in my hospital bed. I suddenly felt a hand holding mine, and I thought I was being taken from this world. In the dim light, I looked up to see my doctor holding my hand. He had come to see me. He was very worried and could not sleep; he came to see how I was doing. Doctors are special people and they have a very tough job. I was fortunate enough to have one of the extra special doctors. As I looked at him, I knew he was giving everything to me and I had to give him my best efforts. Being afraid is awful, but dying is worse. He was a hard man, but it seemed he was concerned.

I was riding an emotional roller coaster. I experienced moments of great relief only to come down almost as hard, and the pain tortured my body. I was really afraid. My body ached from the chemo. I wouldn't look into a mirror as my hair fell out, but I wouldn't let anything stand in my way of beating the cancer. Luckily, I only lost half my hair so I was able to still look OK.

The diary got intense as it told of the pain the chemo caused and the fear of not surviving that filled my mind. All I had wanted was a baby, and now I had lost that and maybe my life as well. This was the low point of the battle; I was really in a bad way. It was at this point I realized that I was fighting because I wanted to have another baby. That was the light I was seeing in my soul.

The fourth chemo would be the strongest dose I would have. It was really an all-or-nothing situation; if it didn't work, it could have taken my life. Many times, it creates a massive heart attack, but it seemed there was very little choice. Die in a month or die with the chemo . . . Not much of a choice. I guess I thought it was worth a try.

Outside the hospital, I spent time at the beach, thinking, absorbing, and smelling the fresh wind on my face and the way you can wake up again to see all of this. Mind set I can do this . . . I can

The day of the chemo, I was weak and upset. To tell the truth, I was scared to death it would fail and I would never wake up. I would lose all that I wanted.

When it was over, the doctors said I was looking very good. The chemo had started to work. I had to have many more, but it was working. That was an amazing feeling, kind of cheating death. I lay in the bed thinking about how I had won the fight and I was going to try to beat the cancer. I remember hearing those words: "It's working." *OMG, that is unreal,* I thought. This gave me the edge I needed.

I had made a friend in the hospital; I bet her that I would make it out before she did. She had laughed at me, saying her cancer was found in early stages so she would be fine and beat me out and that I would die. I did beat her and I will never forget the excitement of doing that. I was so proud of myself, but still afraid. She and I had a private race going on to beat each other. I was impressed at the competition. We would meet and run for the race to our rooms.

I didn't know what lay ahead for me. I decided to fight alone because I didn't want people feeling sorry for me. This was a really good choice. I had no one pressuring, just the pressure I applied to myself. But the friend in hospital, a little fun competition never hurt . . . Giggle makes you want to win.

I was able stay in a positive place if people were not saying bad things to me. I wanted to lock fear out. Because when you are afraid, I think it can make things worse.

It was during this time there were many dark moments at the hospital. It was so bad that those dark moments almost did me in as the fear and confusion pounded in my head. I would lie in the bed and ask myself again and again, "Why? Why? Why?" The nightmares stay in your head.

I cried often, sometimes from pain and other times because I feared I would die. I could hear others crying. We were all in the terminally ill ward, even though I was getting better by the day. I overheard an old lady say, "No one gets out of there alive." I was frightened. I was the youngest patient in the ward and it was really awful. Every Friday I was in the hospital for my treatment, I always felt unwell and tired from the treatment.

The chemo regime was rough on me. It was painful and it caused changes in my body, which cannot ever be repaired. It burnt my throat and has caused my nose to run all the time. Many of my nerve endings have been burnt. I was blowing, wiping my nose all the time, which made me self-conscious always turning and looking to see if people were looking at me. I found ice cream a nice treat at this time, as well as a walk on the beach. The calm atmosphere surrounding me. Happy thoughts! *Gee, it's hard though.*

I attended work, parties, shopping, and everything I needed to do. It was good for me being in a place that makes time go quickly and I was just like everyone else. People around me—I knew they didn't know about the chemotherapy, but still but I was always thinking about it and thinking how they would react if they knew I had cancer and was involved with a battle for my life.

I could hear complete strangers in my mind saying, "I am so sorry. How long do you have." This would bring tears to my eyes and I would respond by thinking, *You don't know me. I'm a warrior. I am fighting, and I will win.* The proof is that I am still here. I have won my battle.

The doctors told me (later in my life) that I have a cancer gene and that is why I had cancer. When I first had cancer, I thought I was just "unlucky," but in the long run, I was lucky. Like following a road map, the road I was on was leading to cancer and I didn't know it. We know that cancer is in the family, and I pray my sisters will not be on the same path.

No matter what has happened, from every bad thing comes something good. The bad thing is you might die if you just give up. The good is that modern science has come a long way and continues down the path of reaching out to you, holding your hand, and providing hope. It is your responsibility to take that hand and work with your doctors. There is always something positive. Look at me. I'm still here, and I plan on being around a long time.

Only my mum, dad, and Ian, and one girlfriend (Deanne Freeman) knew what I had gone through. One lucky thing was I had the best cancer doctor in Australia. Dr. Jok Murray came out of retirement to help me becoming case number 501. I am in a trial book somewhere, and they continue tracking my progress and success.

I can feel all the pain when I think back. I am really lucky. I miss the little girl I lost, even today, and am grateful in some strange way that she saved my life and has given me the power to live a full life and produce wonderful boys. She would have had her birthday on the twenty-third of November or near that. I had named her. It was really hard to let go. I am not really sure that I ever can.

I offered my support to local charities like the Look Good Feel Better program and told the ladies of my voyage after the first battle with cancer. It's painful and yet amazing how much strength can come from a really bad situation when you can help people who are sick and they smile and touch your hand. I realized that is this why we go through terrible times—to survive and help others. This is the truth about surviving; there is a reason some survive and others don't, and those that survive are destined to reach out to others and help them find their way. This is now and was and continues to be my destiny.

I was not allowed to become pregnant immediately; the doctors said wait six months at the least. This seemed like such a long time to me, but the minute I got clearance from the doctors, we began to try again for a child. They never told me I would never have children. But this was what they thought. My cancer was so rare that there was a one in 600,000 chance of getting it.

I was so happy both because I enjoyed our lovemaking and because we were trying to create a life again. I would look into Ian's eyes as we made love and see his happiness, which was within me as well. I was feeling the joy and pleasure of being loved. I found that snuggling in Ian's arm, my head on his chest after we made love, was a wonderful feeling for me. I had escaped the cancer and we were going to create our family.

We were surprised to find out in late 1989 that I was pregnant again. I prayed that everything would go well for us and I would have a lovely child to love and care for.

27

My pregnancy was not hard this time, and I found I was enjoying the idea of having a baby. Of course, my body changed as the baby continued to grow in me and my breasts became huge. I would look in the mirror and see my rounded belly and large breasts and couldn't wait to greet my child. I was afraid though; every pain till after five months worried me so much.

How exciting is that—I got another chance for my baby! Doctors thought I would never have children and here we go, another chance . . . I said, "I am the luckiest girl in the whole world."

Being pregnant was amazing. I loved every single minute . . . even not seeing my toes.

It was September 1, 1990, Father's Day when I gave birth to Nathan Andrew, our first son. He weighed in at seven pounds and six ounces and was absolutely perfect. He was amazing. I sat in bed holding him and feeling his little body, and I was as proud as I could be. It was the most wonderful thing to feed from my breasts, and at last, I felt like a real mother. I was so glad I could nurse him and feel the bond continue between us. He was very demanding and wanted to be fed as often as he was hungry, and of course I was just in heaven when I held him and nursed him. I breastfed Nathan until he was eighteen month old. To my surprise, I became pregnant while I was still breastfeeding Nathan.

They said on the mini pill you would not fall pregnant. Oh, dear, they were wrong. I was so excited: another baby.

My second son arrived on February 27, 1992. Damian Adam weighed six pounds and eleven ounces and was just eighteen months younger than his older brother. Like Nathan, I breastfed Damian. I now realize the emotional bond that was created by breastfeeding my children. It was a joy to watch them nursing, and it built inside me a bond that can never be broken. I always enjoyed looking at them and seeing the joy in their eyes as they suckled my breasts. Like his brother Nathan, Damian was just perfect. He too enjoyed me breastfeeding him for eighteen months before the arrival of my third son. I had become pregnant just after I stopped breastfeeding him.

My family is growing. I have the perfect life. Everything I could ever want, I have. Life is incredible . . . awesome . . . fun.

Branden Alexander arrived on April 26, 1994. He was the smallest of the three, weighing just six pounds, and I thought he was so small. I breastfed Branden for eighteen months as well. At last, we were a complete family; although I had wanted four children, it was not to be. Would you believe that Branden was breech? He had to be a Caesar. I was in a lift accident and it put me in labour. Really weird. Lucky again he was OK and also perfect.

I had been told that if you if you breastfeed your children it lowers the chances of breast cancer. I breastfed all the boys for eighteen months. It was a very hard thing to do, and I nearly stopped several times. My nipples were bleeding a bright red blood. The pain was intense and I cried tears. Mum encouraged me to keep nursing the boys, and after several weeks, it worked. My nipples became tougher and I was OK. I then started to learn how to express milk and freeze it so I could return to work. Ian could feed and I was set to go.

Breastfeeding is very rewarding to both the mother and child, and I feel I gave the boys the very best start to their lives. Of course, there are the anti-breastfeeding mothers who make you feel that if you are breastfeeding outside you are doing something wrong. I wonder what would have happened to this country if the women that settled Australia in the 1800s hadn't offered their breasts to their children. The anti-breastfeeding women are really full on and it's a shame that they really don't understand that it is a natural thing to offer your milk to your child. It's natural and beautiful; my mum fed me for three months when I was born. Women, some however, are sadly not the best supporters for breastfeeding. They say the bottle is easier. Well, I think we should do whatever makes us comfortable. I am happy with what I did.

I remember being at the home of a girlfriend (Susanne Laughton) while breastfeeding Nathan, and a cranky mother asked me to sit inside—even though I was a discreet feeder. Gee, in this day and age, you think they would not care, but there are crazy people around.

Mothers are fantastic, aren't they? Mum and Dad moved in for a while to help me with the boys. It's really exciting learning things from your mum. She had three girls and I had three boys so that was even more special to her. She babysat them every Friday and cooked them whatever they wanted. I think Nathan had his nanny wrapped around his little finger right from the start.

This was a difficult time for me with three boys under three and half running, crawling, and being carried, but I would not change one second of that time. It truly was a delightfully fun experience. When they cried, they all cried. It was funny because I love them so much I really didn't mind them crying because they just wanted me to love them more and more. Now that I think about it, it was like having a little kindergarten in my house. It was the boys first, everything else second. The boys were, and are even today, so fantastic, so affectionate to me. It was a dream come true and it still is. I had the morning teahouse. I invited lots of mums around so we could care for our babies together. We even put a pool in so we could swim. Ian never wanted a pool, but I loved it and so did the boys and the visitors.

My boys are my world, my life, and I will love them with a passion only a mother can feel.

As my boys grew, another part of my life began to crumble. Ian and I were growing apart. After a one-year separation, we finally parted on April 1, 2001. Even though we were divorced, we remained friends and he was one of the first men in my life to come to my aid when the second cancer began. He was supportive and wonderful.

Life throws things at you sometimes; I had wanted a baby since I was thirteen. I babysat for my mum's best friend when I was young and I loved being with her children. Unfortunately for my mum, the friend turned on her in later life. Friends, they are awesome. But some become hard work.

I had a passion to be a mother; it was my top priority as I grew up, and if you have a miscarriage, it turns your life upside down. You are filled with pain both mentally and physically. It is hard times for a woman young or old. Yes, you can tell yourself, "I can have another baby," but that memory still lingers in you. It's never the same. I still think of my girl.

I would watch women at the pharmacy and see how terribly they treated their children. I would feel the anger inside grow as they had no problems delivering their children and I, a woman wanting a baby, was without. I knew I could be a wonderful mother and would provide my children with a wonderful life. I had no child to teach to walk and talk. It was a terrible feeling. I wondered if it was to be, and each time tears streamed down my face. This is hard for any woman. I feel so lucky now though.

But now when I look on my three boys, I know how enriched my life has been. They have helped to make my life complete. I realize that when I lost my first baby, the little girl, she really saved me to be here and have my three boys. I didn't realize this as it was happening. Only now do I understand, and I smile within as I touch the faces of my boys that she is there with us. I look back in amazement of all the great things that have come from this voyage, this journey.

Good journey!

CHAPTER FIVE

Cancer Returns: A New Battle Begins

History repeats itself. In July 2008, tests come back with evidence that a new cancer had returned. I felt like someone shot me! I believed it was an error, but the doctors reassured me that it was cancer. I had breast cancer. My worst fear leapt up into my heart; the diagnosis was true. You hear it and you read it, but you can't believe it could happen twice or even once. My mind raced while recalling the past battle. I prayed that it would be OK. A small part of me had been prepared for the bad news. I think it is silly to think everything would be OK, especially since the disease, the gene, is in the family. I believe it's in our family. Once while visiting Egypt with my friend, Ann Arthur, we stayed with family and after dinner had a discussion and some research. I discovered a history in my family in Cyprus. I learned we have a history that dates back six generations, back when doctors did not know as much as now. They said our relatives died of ladies problems. We believe this to be breast, ovarian, and uterine cancers. We now know that a full genetic testing has to be done to save the future generations and allow them to be aware of what they must do to prolong their lives. Of course, not everyone in a family is affected, but when your number is up, it is up. I have a gene my sisters don't have. My boys will be tested for it. We have a professor and he has done a family tree.

I think my mum was a great fighter, but when she was hit by two battles at the same time, it was just too hard on her. During her battle, I watched as my dad's love poured out to her, how he supported her every moment. He fought the battle as she fought the battle 24/7. He was super husband and lover to her.

I was there a lot loving my mother. When a member of family is ill and you know he or she is dying, the world stops and you have to make allowances for whatever you feel. I supported my dad at this time, but maybe it wasn't enough. Mum had heart disease and ovarian cancer; her biggest asset, her heart, was giving her grief.

My mum was special to me. She was there when I was small child protecting me from real and imaginary problems. She was there to make me happy and support me, to lend a hand with the kids, and to be a shoulder to cry on. She was there to be happy for you when you have great news and when you don't have any great news.

I will tell you it's lonely, sad, and empty, a pure sadness when she is gone. I guess I felt this pain. I looked at my three boys. If I were to die, how would they be without me? They have a great dad, but that is a very different role. A mum's tender kisses, her full support, and her protection—that's what I give to my children, just as she gave it to me.

When she passed away, I lost that, as did my sisters. I always thought Mum would be here forever and ever. I know she would never intend to leave us, but she died young at fifty-three. Not one day passed that I didn't have something happy to share with her.

Now, when there is a special event or occasion, I wish I could share it with her. To see her smile or laugh and knowing that would bring a smile to my face. Those happy and precious moments that I cannot share with her because she is gone are always in my heart. At the same time, the sad moments of fear, when I know she would have closed her arms around me and my family and provided some words of wisdom and hope, are also gone. People who still have their mothers cannot understand this feeling.

I have a special bond with my sisters. We are very close. Our families are growing up now.

In my first cancer battle, my mum was there. The second, I had lost her loving support, which was so really important. All of a sudden, you realize the battle which lies ahead must be faced alone, without her loving protection. At that moment, you realize the darkness that lies ahead for you. I realize today that life is precious, not that I did not already know that but I had taken it for granted. That is something I will never take for granted again.

My mum would be so proud of me and what I have accomplished. I have raised three handsome boys, and I have survived two big battles with cancer. I am now helping others with their voyages. I know she is smiling down on me, as she knows the battle I am fighting. She also knows that I would never leave my kids. That drives me on to be bigger, better, and stronger goals. Not one moment do I ever forget where I came from and what a lucky girl I am. I am lucky. I am here!

I fought the second battle with everyone knowing. Friends were unreal: some shoulders to cry on were offered by acquaintances, but how can you expect a healthy person to know this voyage? We live in a world of know-it-alls. Some women thought they knew how I felt but didn't have a clue. Some friends were of great value, but some were worth no value at all. Still the world continues to spin with problems, and in a way, it was good. I wanted the world to stop, but it doesn't. Whatever your fate, the world keeps spinning.

I had to make some big decisions. My son, Branden, was instrumental in my decisions; my boys were rocked by the diagnosis. Since we had lost my mum thirteen years ago, I think it was really hard for them. I know they must have thought, *Will our mum die?*

It was very hard for me to take it in myself, but even harder to tell my three boys the news. I always promised myself that if I got cancer again, I would give up and die, because the first battle was really hard to chew. But when I sat and watched my children in front of me, I knew I couldn't just give up and die knowing they needed me. I lost my mum when I was thirty-two.

The pain I experienced with her loss made me feel the loneliness of life. A mother is a power figure, one that is supposed to be there forever. I could not be selfish and just cash in my chips. I did not want my kids to suffer the same fate. I could not allow them to feel that loneliness I had felt when my mother died. So in that moment, sitting on the lounge with a bourbon bottle in my hand to try to block the pain, I decided that I would fight and fight hard, and today I am still fighting. The decisions are hard and the whole world has an opinion about how they would cope with the problem. Everyone knows someone who has this disease, and each person becomes an expert on what he or she should do.

Don't listen to them. How in the hell would they know how you feel? They have no clue. You know more about it because you are living it. I realized at this point my way is best. How I am feeling is right. The next thing is blocking that out and standing on your own two feet. This was the only way for me. But I still couldn't make the decision.

Who would ever imagine that at 4 p.m. on the twenty-seventh of July, 2008, I would be on the lounge, lost, afraid holding onto a bottle of bourbon like it was my last best friend. Holding it so tightly, fearing that if I released it my world would collapse. I drink from a glass with bourbon and ice to numb the pain! I had just found out *I have breast cancer*, and it was a mass that had gone undetected. I fell apart. I had battled and won one battle, but with this news, I lost strength to fight. God, how could this could have happened a second time?

Three weeks prior to the lounge day, I had found a lump in my right breast, which was rather sore. A friend had told me if it is sore, that wasn't serious.

I went to my doctor to check it out. He performed a mammogram and an ultrasound and later called me to his office to give me the terrible news. The mammogram had confirmed a cyst. He felt it was OK, but he wanted to do an ultrasound, to be certain. My heart was pounding as fear raced through me. God, what fear does to a person. People tell you to relax and not to worry, to wait for the final results. People handle fear in many ways; they cope with it. I have never been able to cope with fear. It overcomes me. Later, I found that many of my friends and family can't cope with fear and reached out to each other using flowers, religious books, and notes which were sent to my home.

My kids became suspicious seeing my behaviour and all the things arriving at the home. A new battle was just beginning, and I didn't have control over myself and what I had to do . . . I had to survive.

It wasn't long after that I tossed the bourbon in the trash and set myself back on the course of winning the battle. I knew it would require chemo again, and I hated the thought of losing my hair again, but I had to be here for my children. The battle was on, and Nina was going to win it.

I guess the decisions we make are to survive and live! I guess as frightening as it is, the old rule applied for me. The biggest and hardest decision should be the right one. I cried for three days, scared and thinking, *No pain. Take the easy way out do the lumpectomy. Short time out and then quickly back to normal life.* I decided really quickly, *I should do it quickly and move along.*

The doctor told me a single mastectomy was the way. That frightened me as I didn't want to lose my breast. So lumpectomy was the way to go. We booked the operation room and I headed home. However, after coming home, I talked to several people. When I told them I was going to have a lumpectomy, they were horrified and told me I would die. Many lives have been lost by this procedure, and I guess this prompted me to research and look into my decision. This involved reading books and searching the Internet, also talking to people who have lost someone through the cancer battle. Research shows half of those having a lumpectomy were dead as well as a third with the single mastectomy. God, those were not good odds. But that was for under fifty. Oestrogen is dangerous.

Old breast cancer is considered to be in those over fifty. Young breast cancer is under fifty. This seems hard. The older ones mostly survive, or so it seemed. I spent three days non-stop crying and worrying about losing my breasts. I needed to make a decision I could live with!

It was in the afternoon when Branden caught me reading on the lounge about mastectomies. He had surprised me and when he asked what I was reading, I lied to protect him. He looked me right in the eyes and said, "Please, Mum, don't lie. You must tell us everything."

Children have far more intelligence than we give them credit for. At that moment, I decided to be open with my special guys; they had to know where I was. Home had been me and the boys for years. They need me, and I need them. On the Monday morning, I decided that I would make that decision and keep it. Whatever it was, it would be would be the final one with no more tears.

When I look back at that moment, I can only say, "How hard was that."

I tossed back and forth that night, and two nights more, knowing I needed solve this urgently. I believe we have a deep family history, so I decided this was a big part of my choice. There were plenty of tears the next three days. It was a hard call to just say simply, "Cut off my breasts. I want to live." I asked my friend Zu, my best friend what she would do. Her answer was simple: it was better to have them removed love, better to be alive. At the football match, someone who knew I was making a very hard decision asked me what I was going to do. I said I was thinking of having a lumpectomy. My friend's mum, Francis, said it's better to have life than your vanity. My friend, Simone, was behind her and agreed. There were more tears that evening. On Sunday, before I was to make my final decision, I went to bed without deciding what I was going to do. I was in a state of limbo still afraid to make the choice that would change my life forever.

Monday morning, when my feet hit the floor, my decision was made.

I decided I was having a double mastectomy! I was amazed, as this was very macabre and I never in my wildest dreams would want my body to be mutilated in this way. But sometimes it's the only way to hit the nail on the head. I was making a choice for life, and if it cost my breasts, then so be it. They are just fatty tissue; they go south with time. Trying to see the funny side is hard.

I told my doctor I was changing my surgery. She was shocked and horrified. She supports breast conservation, so in her mind it was out of the question to head there when one breast was healthy. My friend, Anne Taylor, was with me. She was horrified but a great support person. I was also told the medical system does not support double mastectomy. So the system made me pay, as no doctor or hospital would support this surgery. I told them this was my decision and it was final so I agreed to pay. The bills ran way higher than the said lots of little hidden charges. Cheryl Hatch was with me when we committed to the surgery costs she was also a great support. She was really supportive, as she has also been there.

I am still paying off this debt, but the doctors had to be paid in advance. Debt of over $40,000, but the first surgery $22,000 with all the tests. Medicare gave very little money back as it's elective surgery with double mastectomy and expanders. *Elective.* How the hell can they say that?

My friends pitched in and did two fundraisers to assist me in paying for my surgery. The first one was in Sydney with Zu and Robert—what amazing friends I have. We pulled together and were able to raise $11,500 from an auction of Sydney and Central Coast friends, including Marie, Anne, Kate, Cheryl, Therese, Simone, Dad, and Sydney Trish. Therese drove her van and gave us all a lift. What great girlfriends. I am so touched by them.

Fundraiser 2 on the Central Coast raised $13,000. Simone started this fundraiser for me. She asked for help. Very quickly, my friend, Marie, from Raging Reunions, who I worked with, and my friends jumped to help: Michelle, Narin, Elly, Trish D, Kylie, and Cheryl formed a committee to pull in some money with not much to work with. Bless them, they did it. Jacki, Jemma, Verity, and Karen helped on the night. There were one hundred people at an auction and dance night, which proved to be a lot of fun. The second fundraiser was after the double mastectomy and I was a little embarrassed to step into a room with no breasts and not really feeling good about how I looked. Karen did my hair, and I guess I looked pretty good considering where I was. I was amazed how everyone was happy to see me looking so well that evening. I have fantastic friends. Hard to thank all, but the messages, the e-mails, and all the phone calls made me smile . . . the outings too.

Members of Liberty Church where I attend—and we work helping and feeding homeless children—were fabulous people during my time not working. The support the mothers cooked and offered to help. They touched my heart. Norah, a beautiful soul, died this year. She was amazing, always by my side. It is easy to see that when there are dark times, the support is always there. I have never been good at asking for help, but I have now learned to do it. Reaching out to people when you are trying to be independent is great, because you can't be strong all the time.

Salvation Army was great. Actually, it is the most wonderful charity. Shirley and Faye there were amazing in providing vouchers and food. Shirley is my rock. She and the Salvos have been there to hold my hand. Thank God for the Salvos. Shirley is my guardian angel. I am so lucky to have her and the other volunteers run the Salvos. What an amazing cause. Please give to them; it truly goes to help families and people. What happened to me could happen to anyone!

My approach to chemo was weird. I first unplugged my brain so there was nothing for me to think about, nothing except one thing: survival. Survival was the only thing out there, nothing else to remember or to reach for in my life. I was working toward survival for myself and my children.

It worked for me. I combined alternative and chemo methods, including fresh fruit juices. And my friend, Dasha, God love her, ordered me a juice from America to help body recover. It cost her one hundred dollars. I met her through Zu, another saint.

These were hard times for my children. I guess they saw too much. They saw me down and watched as I battled my way up again. They saw me trying hard, and it made them proud of me. Their love and care for me helped me along the way, giving the extra edge I needed to overcome the disease.

Lots of bad things happen during the chemo, but when you unplug your brain and focus on yourself and getting better, there was success. It might sound selfish, but it was a way to focus on you and you alone. I slept when I needed to sleep and I forgot about things. Bills fell behind, but every day I was getting better and feeling better. When you sleep, you heal. I believe your body tells you what you need, and you need to listen to it.

Chemo is strange. After each treatment, I could taste it, and if I sweated at all, it was in my sweat. And I could smell it. It was really hard and takes a good six months to exit your system. All that time, the odour of the chemo was with me, causing me to remember the event.

There were many dreams during this period that were upsetting— maybe *nightmares* is a better word. One that occurred many times was of me waking and being told, "You haven't got cancer. It was only a joke." I would lie there and cry. I would touch my head that was hairless and know that it wasn't a joke.

When I look back at those dreams and realize how far I have come, a big smile crosses my face. There is a softness that emerges from within me, but at that moment in time, there was no softness. There was only fear and unhappiness for me and my family. My friend, Althea, in Perth said I was her hero and that I made her proud to be a woman. That made me happy, but still the tears and sadness were there. You fight them back and try to stand proud as they think you are, because it is better to look at the wonderful things ahead and not rest on the terrible things that are happening in your body.

Good journey!

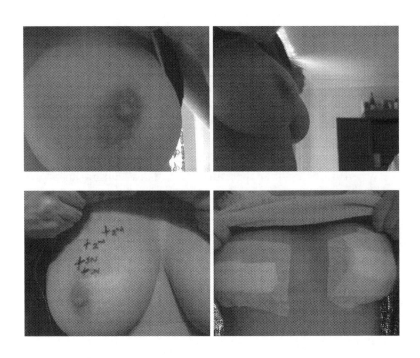

CHAPTER SIX

Surrounded by My Family

Coping with others and telling family a hard voyage indeed. I think when we get bad news we all go into shock. I was numb, hoping I was asleep and would wake up and be told it was a nightmare. When it settles in you, there are still many more things to do.

You must tell your family. Where to begin this duty is so hard, especially knowing that my mother had passed away in her battle. Sadly, we all have not gotten over watching her being tortured by treatments so barbaric. To see a human go through it was awful.

I told Dad first. This was very hard, and I think he was really shocked by my news. I am sure inside it bought up memories for him that were very dark and sad, but at that time, I needed to lean on him. One thing that I have learned during this battle is it is really hard on you and everyone around you. There is fear for everyone when you are battling cancer. Some will look at you and wonder, *Will she die?* or *What day will she die?* It's such a scary, heartbreaking ride filled with ups and downs and twists and turns. You don't want your family to feel your pain, yet you know they do every day.

On the good side, the roller-coaster ride makes us see the value of family and loved ones. A mother is there to protect her children. Lots of my friends have mothers to look after kids, to do housework, listen, and support them, to bandage a knee, or just to sit and hold them in their laps when they cry.

But what happens when you don't have that motherly aspect around? It can be a struggle day-to-day. I am fortunate that my boys are strong like their mum. They all coped with it. During this time, poor Nathan had deal with his high school certificate while Damian had year 10 school certificate, and of course, on top of that, they had to watch their mother face a life-threatening battle.

It would have been easy if they could have looked into a crystal ball and seen the outcome. We didn't know my outcome; we didn't know the end of the story. The story was written day-by-day. The boys were really scared. I guess Nanny was still fresh in their minds as well. How do you teach kids to be tough, to cope?

They watched me when I was ill some days, and other the days when I was OK, and would get dressed up, waiting to be picked up for an outing. I know they were proud because they told me so. I was becoming a fighter and putting up a great fight.

They were so afraid they asked Ian one day if he thought I would die. He looked at them and smiled and said softly, "No, she won't. She will be OK." Deep inside, he knew as I did, and with those few words, he lifted some of the fear from the boys.

My sisters were amazing as they both left their families to be by my side for double mastectomy. They stayed for a week later as well. They even came back a few weeks later.

I remember when I went to the toilet but didn't have the strength to pull up my pants. It was at that time that Belinda, my youngest sister, came into the bathroom after driving more than three hours to visit with me. She rushed past as I begged to have her help me with my pants, saying she really needed to use the toilet. So there I stood, pants around my ankles and my sister using the toilet behind me . . . She and I laughed so much. It was so funny, as I had been half-naked for about twenty minutes and was very frustrated because I lacked the strength to pull them up because of the surgery. In that moment, it wasn't funny, until I looked back at her sitting on the toilet and broke out laughing, and she joined in, laughing harder than I was laughing. Yeah, there are funny days even when you are facing a world of hurt.

Alana, my other sister, walked with me after each chemo and supported me through scary times, both physically and mentally. When they weren't with me, their daily calls supported me and made me feel loved and cared about. I am so grateful to the girls.

I will never forget that, even though we live far apart and even though we have no mother with us, I was lucky to have them there for me. We had each other; we were bounded by blood and our love for each other. We were entwined, inseparable. I think they were afraid for me, but they saw how well I was coping and it gave them peace of mind. We talked and laughed. We remembered the past. We recalled all the good times at the beach or by the river. We were like little girls at a slumber party.

After the surgery, Dad put me up at his house. This was amazing to spend time with him. One week he cared for me.

It was so nice having his support. He was an amazing man, father. Coming home and being cared for, nurses came daily and life was restful. They boys missed me but came up and back to see me daily.

So you see, family is so important. It's a support that is crucial, and as I look back today, I am grateful for the love and support they gave me in my life and through my illness. My boys needed me and I had to be here for them. I am a proud woman and asking for or receiving help is a hard thing for me to handle. It is one thing to reach out your hand and ask for assistance. It is another to wake each day to see a smiling face asking you how you are and if there is anything they can do for you. I understand now that sometimes we need help and we have to ask, but when people are there without being asked it's unreal.

When it came time to discuss what lay ahead for me with the children, Ian and I decided to lolly-coat it so they could deal with it as best as they could. The boys were seventeen, sixteen, and fourteen.

I called a meeting in the kitchen, I stood looking at them and quietly said, "Boys, Mum has been quite upset, but everything is OK. I have breast cancer, but we think we have found it early and

I will be OK after the operation and all will be back to normal." It is hard to tell your children how really bad it is. How do you tell them that you might die? How do I tell them they might be taken away from me?

They stared at me in amazement, and I know in their minds they were reliving the memories of losing their grandmother to ovarian cancer. They didn't say anything. Overcome with emotions, they walked away thinking about what might happen to their mother.

As they walked away, I sighed with relief thinking about the horrible thing I had just dropped in their laps. In a way, I was relieved that they finally knew what was happening with their mother.

I was still standing at the kitchen table when Branden appeared alone minutes later. "Mum will you die?" he asked.

I was so shocked. I smiled at him and said, "I don't think so. I'm strong and I can do this."

He responded, his voice wavering, "How do you know? Others haven't made it."

I pulled him into my arms, holding him tightly as I assured him I would be fine. We stood holding each other as tears welled-up in my eyes and he walked away.

As I watched him leave, I wondered how this story would be written, how the ending would be. No one at that moment knew. I was so afraid of leaving three boys without a mother. I knew that death was something that will happen to us in our life, but we hope it takes place when we are old and in our sleep. At that moment, I knew breast cancer might take that away from me. I could not allow that to happen.

I had a really big cry in the kitchen while sitting at the table, before going to my bedroom. Flopped onto the bed and grabbed my pillow and began to punch it, crying softly, "No, no, no, don't take me, please!" My mind raced. *Why me? Why like this?*

Between the crying and punching my pillow, I drifted off to sleep, and then woke half an hour later. I was angry, upset, and worried about what lay ahead and tossed and turned in an uneasy sleep.

When I awoke, my mind raced ahead seeking answers that couldn't be answered right then. Will I be OK? I knew I had to make it. I had to show my boys that I was going to recover.

I lost my mother and I knew how empty it had been without her; life without a mother is really horrible. I had watched her die a slow, horrid death, and my head suddenly was filled with the nightmares that had begun with her slow death. Now I was facing my own fight, an even bigger war a war of my own. I cried out in the darkness, "Help me! I am afraid." But I can do this. I *can*.

When I was diagnosed in July, half my time was spent doing tests and such, so my income was halved. I was self-employed and if I didn't work, there wasn't money to pay the bills. Yet because of all the testing, I had to turn away work. It wasn't long before the bills were piling up and debt collectors were hounding me. Even when you told them what was happening, they didn't care at all. After seven months of no work and nearly losing my house to the bank, I had no money but still the voyage continued. I was too proud to ask for help. Although Ian helped me with money, it seemed never to be enough. It's hard being so vulnerable. I am so grateful to family and Ian for their support.

When I got back to work, I was very busy and loved it. However, I had to sell my house cheap so the bank would not take it. There were many dreams that have been slashed through this voyage, but I have made new dreams and always there is a way to get through. I began paying off medical bills and catching up on my other bills, but still it was really hard. Charity and church gave us food and some vouchers, which was a great help. Still, I am very independent and not having money was really awful. It was hard imagining no breasts, no hair, no eyebrows, no eyelashes, and no money, but I survived it all. Life is always good no matter what curves are tossed at you. My breast cancer battle was a financially and mentally straining time. It turned my life inside out, but when I look in the mirror, I am so proud of where I have been and where I am going. I look and feel great. I have no fear, and I know as hard as it's been that I have made the right choices. With cancer, whether you have a health fund or not, you will pay big money!

I found friends helpful after my surgeries. When I couldn't lift my arms, they would help to undress me and dress me. Those were difficult times for me and my family. My body and mind were in a bad way. I sat there, body racked with pain and feeling terrible inside, the tears streaming down my face, and yet I knew with the help of my boys I would pull through it all and come out the winner. I was going to be a survivor no matter what roadblocks were placed in front of me. I had to make it for my boys.

I found that keeping sailing with my mates Graham, Bard, Stuart, and George, and going out for lunches with friends, was important, positive, and getting to appear normal. This was important to me. When I could, that's what I did.

I had one morning where I could not stop crying; my body and mind were in a very bad way. I was torn apart, but then I wondered why all the tears. I had to pull myself together for my boys. In November, we started chemo this would further delay going back to work. As I began the chemo, I promised myself that I had to regain my health first.

I thought that since I had chosen a double mastectomy, I would dodge the chemo bullet. I was to learn how wrong I was. Yes, I had the option to refuse the chemo, and many do, but I worried that if I did, I wouldn't live to see my grandchildren. When the doctors and I talked chemo, the very word made me sick to my stomach. I wanted to cry but could hardly do anything. I needed to complete the surgeries and get it out of my head.

As I drove away from the meeting, the farther I drove, the more in shock I became. I stopped at a grocery store to purchase milk. I saw my friend Jemma. As I sat behind the wheel of the car, I felt numb and lost. I began to cry, not caring if people saw me or wondered about why I was crying. This was my second round with chemo, and I knew once I began that there was no turning back.

My brain was rocked with the single thought: *Chemo again. Oh, God, please help.*

Disgusting memories of my first battle with chemo washed over me again and again. My soul was flooded with the sickness, the vomiting, and the pain. My emotions overcame me and I felt lost, alone, and very tired, even though the treatments were yet to start. Just how could I do it again? How could I stand up to everything that had before? Did I have the strength?

I listened to the doctors tell me that chemo had changed over the years and it wasn't as bad. I had to accept what they were saying about chemo, that patients were tolerating the procedure better and the new drugs to help stop vomiting. He had found all types of drugs for this pain.

Still sitting in the car, I was able to repress the tears, and I looked into the rear-view mirror and made my decision right then. Hell! I can do this, and if what they say is true, it may work.

I was administered in chemo for half a day every three weeks. Chemo was one red in colour and one white. The doctors talked about cycles, and it would conclude with four. *Four*, I thought, *I can do that, double doses*. It wasn't easy. After each one, my body felt flogged. Red one is called the red devil.

The first chemo cycle, I was down for two days; by the final cycle, I was down for two weeks. Each cycle sent me down more and more, hitting me harder and harder.

There were up times during each cycle when I would go out and have fun, but when I was sick, I would simply close the curtains and rest on the lounge. These were times for me and my body to commune. Sometimes, I sat there and cried inward and outward, and sometimes, I realized there was a reason for all that was happening. I wasn't just doing this for myself. I was doing it for my boys as well.

Of course, my hair fell out completely and quickly. It starts coming out in large clumps. You know it's going to happen, but it's very hurtful. If I brushed my hair, it came out in clumps. If I just ran my hands through my hair, it came out. I was afraid and upset. Even the nurse who came to shower me passed me a rather large clump of hair.

My advice for others, since this really hurts a woman when she holds her hair in her hands and it isn't on her head, is to look to the future when it returns and how it was before the chemo. Forget about the bald spots and stay positive. I remember how my head got so hot and would cook my hair to my head. It was really disgusting and very upsetting. Two of my friends, hairdressers Robert and John, told me to cut the hair short, but an inner voice told me I could keep my hair if I wanted it. Of course, this was wishful thinking and never was to be.

I finally had Marie, a friend, cut off the burnt pieces, and I grabbed a hat and headed to Sydney by train where my friend Zu picked me up from the central station to take me to a salon.

As we were drove in her convertible, my hair was flying away. Although I couldn't see it flying away, I knew it was happening, and tears came to my eyes. My feelings were hurt. People stared, and I know that was a hard day on Zu, yet she was unreal through this battle. She is my saviour. She never lied to me. She always called it as it was. I know this was a hard day for her. One person told me she never lost her hair, so I hoped that would be me . . . ."Cut your hair," "Avoid this," "Bald is OK," "Girls' wigs are fabulous." I had three and I changed them around. Fancy that no more bad hairs days, if you get what I mean. I had to see the funny side. I love my hair.

When we got to our special hairdresser, John, he hugged me and we talked as he held my hand. He listened and we decided to shave off the remaining hair. At that point, I was nearly bald anyway. He used his shears to remove the last remaining strands. As I sat in his chair, we both cried. We had worked so hard with my hair, and he had helped to make it so beautiful, and yet in just a few moments, it was totally gone and I sat looking at a bald lady. I looked strange, and I thought I was very ugly.

The tears came again, but John and Zu comforted me. When we left the salon, I remember feeling very scared as drove away. I wondered how strange I must look to other women on the streets.

By the second month, my eyelashes were gone, and if I looked into a mirror, I looked really strange. When the third month rolled, around my eyebrows became the next casualty as they began to fall out. When I only had half of the eyebrows, I tried drawing them on, but the pencil only succeeded in removing what was left of my eyebrows. You reach a point when you don't want to look into a mirror because your skin goes grey and under your eyes starts to turn black. You look old and in a way evil because of all the greys and blacks covering your face. It finally reached a point where I was afraid to look in the mirror and even more afraid to see my appearance getting worse and worse as the chemo continued.

The second night after chemo was perhaps the worst night of my life. I didn't sleep very well, even though the tablets I was taking to stop the vomiting worked very well. But I still had the urge to vomit and I wanted to, but then it would pass. You're tired. You look awful and feel really sick. You whole body aches with pain, and it throbs. I had a high fever and wasn't myself at all. Weeks later, on a Sunday, I looked in the mirror and wondered, *Who the hell is this person?* I had no memory of what I was or who I was. All I saw was this dreadful, sick, awful-looking person looking back at me. I thought I had died for sure and no one had bothered to tell me I had died. I was convinced that anyone who looked so awful like I did must have died. I realized that couldn't be true as I was in terrible pain, a really deep pain all over. I put my hand on my neck. It felt like my hand went into my body, and it was hot and intense.

As I lay in the bed, moving my hands from place to place and feeling the heat radiate, I knew I wasn't dead. I glanced into the mirror again and I smiled. "You cannot be in this much pain if you are dead." I smiled and smiled, got out of bed, and moved to the lounge. I thought, *I am still here. How lucky is that. I am being flogged and I'm still alive. It may hurt, but I'm still here so I can take all that can be dished out.* It was a strange feeling. you find it hard to see yourself like that: beat up but still a winner as you are surviving. I remember hearing a little bird chirping outside my window. I thought, *I will go out there and smash him with a brick . . .* Then I thought, *He is so happy singing, it must be a lovely day*, and that made me so happy. Actually, thinking of the little bird made me smile all day. I still think of my friend the bird. I wonder where he is now! He is lucky he is alive.

When I got to feeling better and not so beaten down, my friends Michelle, Jacki, Karen, and Adelene took me to the club for lunches. Going out to eat with my friends was a highlight of a day. It was very exciting to get dressed up, put on my shoes and wig. I always selected my best wig for these occasions. It's really important not to forget who you are at this time. I would spend some time getting ready: applying make-up, drawing eyebrows, and using eyeliner to mimic mascara. When I finished, I always looked like a million dollars. Actually, when I see photos of myself at this time, it is hard to imagine how sick I was, but at that time, I knew just what I was going through and I knew just how unreal I looked. I was excited to be picked up and be free from my house, which was appearing more like a sick bay. When I sat and watched people and had a lunch and a laugh with the girls, I would apply my lipstick and try to feel I was normal and just out having fun, even laughing like my old self. I would think, *Wow, I can do this. I know I can. I am so proud of how I did this.*

Yes, I still felt sick still, but that was my secret. I wanted people to see me because that made me feel good inside. Those moments are the best you can ever feel when you are in the middle of a battle for your life. We sometimes forget the little things in life. But when I reflect on this journey, I remember those wonderful phone calls I got as a cancer patient. I remember text messages or e-mails which made me warm inside and brought a smile to my face. Even when the world you are living in seems at its dark point, it's wonderful to know people out there that want to bring a smile to your face and keep your world spinning and make you hold out for the next day, week, or month.

My boys saw me during this period being so very sick. They were with me when I was well up and about doing things with them; they saw my determination to survive; they were happy that I was able get back up after being knocked down. There was always warmth in their kisses, smiles that made me smile, kindness when they needed to help me, and urging me on every day.

The last chemo was delayed a week because my body stats were low, and I waited. It was a very exciting point in all the hell I had been living with, and I could barely wait for it to finally end.

The last chemo was completed at the end of January 2009. By March, my hair was starting to grow back. It is so wonderful to run your hand through your own hair and not have any in your hand when you finish. I loved it when I could sail and have the wind blow my hair and the happiness that I felt from that one simple thing. I began to feel more like the woman I once was and headed for the woman I would become when I would face the surgeries that lay ahead. Again, it is the little things that make you feel good, how special that day was for me.

When I finally had a full head of hair, I was elated. My hair grew back black and curly, just like a golliwog—about eight shades darker than it used to be. It was horrid, but isn't that what hair dye is for? It is another amazing miracle of science. I got back to being a blonde easily. You should see me now. My hair is nearly down to my shoulders. It's soft and very beautiful, just like it used to be. Oh, wow, and dyed blonde. Well, I am loving it.

Here I must thank Peter, my hairdresser. We have a joke we are the Will and Grace of the Coast. "My gay husband" became my nickname for him. I love him; he was wonderful friend while I was sick taking me to dinner, washing my hair, and of course making me blonde again. OMG, that black curly hair was awful. I thought my pubic hair had grown back in the wrong place. *Eeeekkkk!*

Actually, all kidding aside, I am grateful for my hair growing back strong and thick. My eyebrows also came back, even though they are a bit patchy. My eyelashes are unreal. They came back and I now consider mascara my favourite thing. It's exciting as you get back that which you have lost; there are times in losing these things I thought maybe I was turning into a boy. These were very hard moments. I was breastless, hairless, and in pain, but I always stayed set on my goal to survive. I am glad I did, when each morning I look in the mirror and see the reward I have.

I always kept this in mind as I moved on: "I am strong, I can do this, I am still a woman, and I can get new ones." There should always be a moment of laughter in any statement one makes. It's always a mental game you have to play. How much do your looks mean to the way we feel about everything as a whole? When I was at the bottom of the barrel and looked in the mirror, I looked like a toad, but I came back stronger and more determined. I am as precious a princess as I ever was. I am loved and make people smile, just as many of them made me smile when I was at the bottom of the journey.

I remember the day I told Marie I had breast cancer. She saw it in my eyes. She was lighting a smoke. I said, "Can I have one?" She said, "You don't smoke, love." I said, "I have nothing to lose. Give me one." We laughed and cried so much. "Bourbon girls," I call them for obvious reasons. Marie and Kylie were amazing. Those girly parties made me happy. The girls are like family.

You will laugh at this. I have a friend named Althea. She lives in Perth. We met at work. On the phone, we spoke every day. We have never seen each other. We know each other inside out and we tell each other secrets and talk all kinds of trouble and good stuff. Ten years like this—we will meet one day. I can't wait. We giggle and solve problems of the world; we are clever. Many tears and laughter . . . friends forever. She really inspired me to see myself as she saw me! I am strong. I can do this. John supported me at work. Sharone and Kaye were wonderful and then Argie supported me on the phone. You don't have to be there; it's all about the love. I had heaps . . . Support is crucial and wonderful.

Good journey!

CHAPTER SEVEN

Surgeries and Recovery

There were several surgeries I would have, including a hysterectomy, oophorectomy, and a double mastectomy.

Never had heard of one of them. I guess I had, but it was a learning process and very painful as well. I had keyhole surgery through four holes in my abdomen; they removed everything: ovaries, uterus, etc. I elected to have this done. Since my mother had had ovarian cancer, I figured this was best. I was upset and did not want to do this deep down, so worried about being so young. No hormones. What would happen to my hair and my skin? Would I go grey? Would I be OK? Fear. So many horror stories too. Don't you love those scare you way too much and most stories not true. My experience was OK. Pain was quite bad for a while, but I recovered. No symptoms are troubling me. Lucky and happy another good call. My gynaecologist was great. He explained everything and I was very happy because then I would I know what was happening. Some doctors are just like friends; they are fantastic.

The hysterectomy and oophorectomy took place in April of 2009 after I recovered from the chemotherapy, which ran from November to January 2009. The chemo was done in a chair and I was a day patient at the time.

Oophorectomy, or ovariectomy, is the <u>surgical</u> removal of an <u>ovary</u> or ovaries. Oophorectomies are most often performed due to diseases, such as <u>ovarian cysts</u> or <u>cancer</u>, prophylactically to reduce the chances of developing ovarian <u>cancer</u> or breast <u>cancer</u>. Or they are done in conjunction with removal of the uterus. A hysterectomy was completed at the same time. A hysterectomy is the <u>surgical</u> removal of the <u>uterus</u>. In my case, it was the total hysterectomy including the fundus and cervix of the uterus. With the removal of my uterus, I was rendered unable to bear any more children.

Just an update: I am doing fantastic. I have not needed medical intervention. Only symptom is hot and cold flushes . . . That is fantastic, and I feel great.

The double mastectomy was on October 9, 2008. It was my choice to perform the surgery. I knew at the time if I wanted to have my breasts rebuilt, it would take a number of operations to have my breasts back.

The double mastectomy pushed me into early menopause; the chemo pushed me even further in. Women go through a lot, and menopause is something we all face, yet everyone copes differently. The hot flushes can be very bad; water drips from every pore, like a tap, and is very embarrassing. It is weird. When I am warm, I am so hot, and then five minutes later I am freezing cold. Deep down inside, I didn't want to do go through menopause because I was worried about being so young and not having the hormones. I wondered what would happen to my hair and my skin. Would I wrinkle up? Would my hair go grey? Would I be OK in the long run? I had heard so many horror stories which scared me, but most stories were not true. My experience was OK. Pain was quite bad for a while—six to eight weeks actually—but I recovered with no symptoms troubling me. I was lucky, and it made me happy that I had made the right call for me.

The double mastectomy surgery took several hours and four doctors, and two expanders were placed in my breasts. When they finished, I was taken from the operating room to the recovery room. It was four days in the hospital and three weeks of home-care nurse at my dad's, and later at my home. When I left hospital to go to my dad's, I had three drains under my arms: two on the right and one on the left. I was very dizzy and had to have help moving about from the hospital to the car and into the house. I really wasn't with it. Anne drove me. she was wonderful. The nurses came daily to change the wounds and performed a great service, but I was still not really with it and I wished they could have kept me longer at the hospital.

The expanders were filled with 200 millilitres of fluid and I left the hospital an A cup, whereas before the surgery I was a 32 E. Due to the skin being folded back, scar tissue formed on my left breast and a hole appeared on my right breast two months after the surgery. I would have three "refills," adding another 200 millilitres, 250 millilitres, and 200 millilitres, for a grand total of 650 millilitres on each side to create a size D cup. With my clothes on, I looked wonderful, but each time I was naked, I knew I still looked terrible. It was going to take time for the healing to be complete.

The reconstruction of my breasts was just beginning!

Since the goal of breast reconstruction is to recreate symmetric, natural-appearing breasts while preserving patient safety and quality of life, it would take several surgeries with the expanders becoming larger and larger with each fill. The expanders were in eighteen months, and after some daily pain, I got used to them, but they are hard on a person. I lost movement in my arms and shoulders, and they changed my body. I looked at them and touched them and found them to be soft, but without the nipples, they were lacking sex appeal for me.

Of course, there is always a good side to anything. All my life, I have had large breasts, and after the first surgery, I found it enjoyable to not have to wear a bra. When you are busty, you must wear one all the time. I guess body changes are hard. you go from a normal body to one that has been hacked up, and that is hard. When you look at it from the point of view of life versus vanity, I chose life. As my body changed, a part of me was amazed that with my clothes on, no one would ever know what lay beneath. I was still a beautiful woman in the flesh, still a sexy woman. I would walk down a street and men turned their heads, and those were very satisfying moments for me. No one knew that beneath my clothes was a reconstructed woman. I guess that's the beauty we have. If you lose your hair, you can wear a wig. if your eyebrows fall out, you can draw them back on. eyelashes gone? Add a little extra eyeliner and you look just like everyone else. What a wonderful world that we can be nearly new with a little help. No kidding, though there are physical and mental scars. (They go deep. For the experts who say it's no big deal to just cut them off—it's huge to us who have lived it.)

With the surgery, my breasts were expanded. My cup sizes slowly moved up from A to B to C and finally D cup. Each time my breasts were expanded, I had pain as the healing took place. Actually, pain is a good sign, as it tells you you're healing. At each expansion, I would stand in front of a mirror and cup my breasts, feeling their weight and looking at how wonderful they were and how happy I was with each new creation. At each cup size, I began to feel that I had made the right choice in having the double mastectomy. You never know how incomplete a woman feels when she has had her breasts removed. There is fear of thinking you're no longer a woman, that you will never please a man, but when you are going through the reconstruction phase, it is an exciting feeling knowing you are going to have your breasts back.

The March 30, 2010, surgery was the last in the rebuilding phase. It had taken three hours and it was a long recovery for me as I was really under. They had removed the expanders, placing them with prostheses, and I spent two days in hospital recovering.

As I lay in the bed, I was amazed that blood stains your skin. I would wipe it, and it came off. You can't imagine what happens while you are under. There was a bonus for me when I woke up as I found Marelyn, a friend, smiling down at me. We had battled with all the same doctors and we laughed and made jokes to entertain ourselves. It was a blessing to have such good friends who understand and share my demons. We often ate breakfast together, and she has become one of my friends. I think she will always be.

I had a fair bit of bleeding on the right side. they nearly kept me in another night, but they decided there wasn't a need for that. Auburn Hospital was great, new, and the staff was really good to Marelyn and me. I asked for cocktails and they said the cocktail tray would be around at 2 p.m. as they played along with us. Marelyn and I laughed and placed our orders for a cocktail or two. We deserve it.

It is amazing the friends you meet on this voyage. They are strong and willing to support each other in the battle that each faces.

When you have a double mastectomy, it takes ages to use your arms again; my range of motion was very poor for a long time. I started martial arts classes and have a fabulous instructor named Ken. We worked slowly at start and it improved my strength, my range of motion, and my mind. My right side, the cancer side, is a lot tighter than the left, and it took time for it to loosen up.

My other exercise is sailing. I am on the halyards, a crewmember on a sailing team called Divine Intervention. Since I had had chemo, I kept up a brave face, which really gave me a sense of being. When I was without hair from the chemo, the wind in my wig and on my face made me forget a battle was in play. We always came to win the races, and I didn't want that to stop. I love sailing and my sailing mates. We are a crew of five including me. They made my chemo trips and recovery better.

A smile, an outing, a sailing race, a drink out to lunch—all made me feel happy and better, just like the old Nina-Ann I remembered.

Five weeks after the surgery and I was still having some pain, but it was bearable and I suddenly realized how amazing I looked. Standing in front of a mirror with a bra on and V-neck blouse, I was overwhelmed. I was wearing just the blouse and panty as I stood at the mirror. I turned every which way, and I knew I was back. They were like my breasts of the past, same yet different. I closed my eyes and I imagined me in other clothes. I thought about swimsuits and sailing togs. I was starting to feel like I wanted to step out into the world and no one but me would know what lay beneath my clothes. My new breasts looked quite good, but they will never be the same. I love them anyway. I have to have them redone because the skin is now hanging, so in June 2011 that will take place again . . . Then in four months, I am going to have my nipples made. How bizarre and fun. I get to pick them. Oh, and of course, what colour: brown or pink? How exciting.

As I said earlier, I have always wanted to be a Barbie Doll, and now that I am half-plastic in my breast, I have finally gotten the chance. I laugh about it sometimes as it is one of the funny sides of this journey. You always need to see the funny side of any event, even if it is about you. Laugh or cry. I would rather laugh. Look for the positive.

Now, one of the advantages of new breasts at my age is that natural breasts are generally headed south. Women realize that it is just part of growing older, but when I look at mine and see how perky they are, and think that they are almost like when I was younger, it sends a warm feeling through my body. Yes, I am smaller than before. I was an E, which is big. They are so unique. When I wear a low cut or V-neck blouse, no one knows I have had breast cancer. From the top, they look very real.

When I was without hair, I had plastic hair wigs, which are cute but also very uncomfortable. It gets very hot under those wigs. I remember one time when I was at a doctor's office for a general check-up. I was sitting next to a heater and began to feel very warm. I felt like I was beginning to melt, so I moved as far away as I could from the heater. The doctor's receptionist looked up and smiled at me and asked if I was all right.

I smiled back and said, "If I don't move, I'm going to melt. I'm half plastic, you know." It startled her a moment, and suddenly we were both laughing so hard we almost cried. You have to find things that make you laugh. You know what they say: if it is a choice between laughing and crying . . . let's laugh. It feels better.

I did have a concern when I was bald. I knew I needed to return to the ocean and my love of sailing. It is my passion that brings out the best in me. It was a way of doing battle with the cancer; it gave me a goal and filled my desire of winning. Although I do have a very cute bald head, I didn't really want to advertise it to my sailing buddies. My worry was my wig in high seas might be ripped away, revealing my bald head.

Good wigs are not inexpensive, but you can purchase cheap wigs. Just remember you get what you pay for, and you never want to look bad out for dinner or drinks. No matter what wigs I found, they were both itchy and hot. I wore a medical wig, which cost about six hundred dollars. It looked nice, and I had perfect hair every day—a true bonus for a woman. The Wig Library is run by volunteers, and they are very good. Every hospital has one, I believe. A hairdresser fits the wig properly for anyone coming to him or her. People without get an extra bonus, as the wigs are donated to the organization. I plan on donating my wigs to the Wig Library because you never know what's around the corner and it's great to give. When you give from your heart and from the knowledge of what you have gone through yourself, it makes a huge difference. When your hair has grown back and you see someone that you know is wearing a wig, there is a special feeling in you. You have been there and you made it out. You say a prayer for that person and then head on your way.

Being positive and keeping a fun side to the battle is the only real way to survive. Again and again, you have to find the lighter side of the massive problem that rests on your shoulders. Laughter really is the best medicine. Laughing until you cry is greatest healer in the world. Oh, and a glass of wine or two . . . or bourbon.

When I first left the hospital with my A cups, my son Branden was lying on the bed with me reading a book, and suddenly he looked me in the eyes and said, "My friends have bigger boobs than you have now." I laughed and said to him, "Your friends are younger than I am, like thirteen." He smiled and said some were even twelve. We laughed so hard we almost left of the bed.

Kids are unreal and really can make light of a situation. I loved we could laugh together. That made me happy.

I lost some weight, which is expected when recovering from surgeries, and I regained my confidence as the days and weeks passed. My hair grew back and I tried several different accessories and wigs until I selected one I liked the best. The year 2009 had been very tough, but 2010 was super for me. Getting used to a different look.

It's hard having all the scars. My breasts were a creation of my doctors making me a whole woman for the first time in more than two years. I am proud of my doctors and their accomplishments, and I was glad and happy to be a new woman.

We must be willing to get rid of the life we are planning and have the life that is waiting for us.

Good journey!

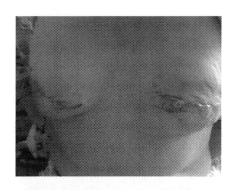

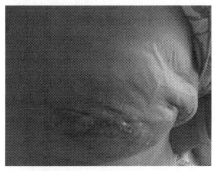

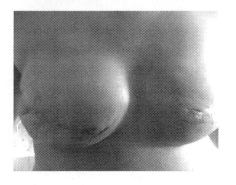

CHAPTER EIGHT

The New Me: Different yet the Same

When I look in the mirror today and see the long hair and hourglass figure, I smile. Before me is a strong yet soft woman. I feel that life and work are really good, and I know I am in a great place.

I am a better sailor now that I have strength back in my arms. I have plugged my brain back in and guess what: I can cope with anything. I am confident dating again. Back at tennis, have to practise a bit here though. Oh, well, it will happen. It may not happen overnight, but it will happen.

I have cleaned out the space or so to speak, no draining people around and most things I don't have to care about I don't. Just spending time with family and friends. I am doing some charity work and would love to help others on this voyage.

I am back . . .

CHAPTER NINE

I Am Still a Woman

I guess it's hard to know what will happen when a doctor says you have cancer; it comes as a huge hit to anyone facing the journey I have finished. In your mind, you say, *Will I die? Will I suffer? Can I really do this?* The answer is you can win the battle, if you are willing to set your mind and body on the course of success.

I was asked about a friend's friend who wanted to kill herself because she could not cope with the cancer she had. The friend wanted my advice as a survivor.

I answered by saying that every cancer sufferer has those same thoughts. I admitted that I had thought about crashing my car into a rock on the freeway because I was afraid I would fail on my journey. But I always found something that kept me from doing it. The desire to live outweighs the desire to die. The thoughts of watching your children marry and bringing your grandchildren home for you to spoil. The thought of watching a sunrise or sunset, the simple pleasures of a warm kiss or the joy of just waking up to another day should be enough to drive you to fight the battle that lies in front of you.

I admit it is a very hard process and the support that you get from friends and family are really important. No one knows what will happen when he might be told this, but there are some know-it-alls, and we all know who they are—those free medical experts that think it is easy. Those individuals who have never faced a terrible disease, who pass out advice as if it were a piece of candy. They don't know and will never know until it happens to them. How can they know?

It's the little things that count. It's a stranger, who has no idea who you are, smiling at you in the street. Living, though, is not a solo journey. It's a hug for no reason from a loved one or friend. It's knowing that in those darkest moments you are not alone, that someone is sending you an e-mail, a text, or a phone call. These are the things that are wonderful, and these are the things that keep you sane and from self-destruction.

I am grateful to family and friends for their support; it's really great how love pours out to you. It is like a huge wave crashing against the shore; it leaves you with something new in your heart wave after wave.

My friends, my dad, and sisters texted or called me every day, which was such a great thing. My children were amazing as well, even though they were worried, upset, and afraid, they were above all to me supportive and helpful.

In life, there are things you can change and things you can't, but if you want to be a survivor, go for it! If there are things that upset you, change them, and the things you think cannot change, go with it . . . Do it!

I have touched many lives since I began this journey, and I have been touched by many others, and that is what life is all about: reaching out and touching as many as you can. Every day is a bonus, whether you are well or ill.

I lost my hair and who cares? I got it back! I had my breasts removed but got new ones back. Life is really a test! You can pass or fail—it is up to you. I have always chosen to pass. Remember everybody touches you in a different way. You need support. Hold out your hand. There is someone waiting to touch you.

I am still a woman—happily ever after . . .

Good journey!

Epilogue

When I look back at my journey, I know it is a hard topic for most women. I realize how unreal and how consuming cancer can be, not only for the woman or man that faces it but the family and friends who are involved—because they either love you or care about you. I found some of my friends there for me and others who turned away and were more concerned with themselves and were self-absorbed. There is an old saying that "a friend will help you kill someone and bury the body; an acquaintance just sits on the fence."

I have looked closely at my female friends. I realize that some were unreal and some were shallow. Before my battle began, I was not sure how it would end or how my friends would be, but I know now the true friends were the ones who had a few drinks with me and laughed and cried with me. They understood the stress levels the pain was having and knew it was not worth getting upset about, that just being there for me was more important. I now avoid the ones that are all about themselves, and I hope they look back on their foolish and stupid statements and realize how self-centred they were. I forgive them.

I say live life; most people know what that means.

To the women in the world who may think they may never have to face this issue, I wish you well. I wish you happiness. To those that have to face it or have already faced it in their life, I want them to remember that I made my choices and I survived. You can too if you have must.

To my male friends who were a pleasant surprise during my battles with cancer, I offer an apology. I had thought you would abandon me. How silly I was to think that, for you were there for me, supporting me from start to finish.

To my sweet sons, who have suffered through it all, including watching their grandmother die of cancer and their mother battle the terrible disease! You are the pillars of strength for me. I am so very proud of you. When I was well, you were there for me. When I was sick on the lounge chair, you were there. When I needed to take a nap, you took one with me. I am proud of you for your support and your courage. You knew I would fight, and you never gave up hope. I saw it in your faces every day. Thank you.

For my ex-husband, Ian, who helped me financially and who I was able to talk with openly. Thank you. You are my rock, and we are the greatest friends. We have different personalities, and we did not make it, but I care about you, and what you gave me financially was unreal.

To my dad, who was a real father for me. You had to battle the memories of Mother's cancer while you cared for me after the operations. I love you so much for that.

According to statistics, 75 percent of men walk out. Well, Dad, you were and are amazing. You supported my mother and I admire you for that. I know my cancer battles upset you as you had to relive Mum's battle again, and I was not sure how you would react, but you were always there for me as a child and you remained there for me as a woman. I love you, Dad!

Other men stood by me during those trying times, including John, who lost his second wife to breast cancer. He believed I could make it, and I did. His wife, Margaret, touched my life as well. They are an amazing couple with amazing support for me. It is funny how he knew I was sick and he supported me by offering his shoulder to cry on. He is like my second dad. We travelled the F3 (freeway) many times. I was able to lean on him. My adopted parents, they are. I adore them. Thank you.

David, who is my close male friend. Call and take me to lunch. He would always ask me how I was feeling, and if I replied I was good, he would he would come back with, "Just how good are you today?" I guess we all like to be strong; he was that for me, a rock. He was the real thing. He is the eternal optimist, and if one looks deep into him, he is the male version of me: a true friend.

Girlfriends, there are way too many to name. You know who you are. Thank you from the bottom of my heart. For the tears the laughter and the quality of being us together forever . . .
Oh, and for singing "I Am Woman" with me . . . Priceless! Also, my sisters. You are the best.

My sailing friends Graham, Bard, Stuart, and George, to mention just a few of the many at the sailing club who have touched my life after I finished the chemo and returned to sailing, a sport that I love so much. The thought of cruising on the waves gave me something to look forward to when I was doing chemo. The guys only found out after how weak was, and they were shocked.

When a woman or a man goes through chemo, support is very important. To be surrounded by friends, loved ones, and family can make the difference in making it or not making it. Fine those who really care about you and understand you, and you will come through with their help and the help of God.

Marie Paterson (a close friend) said this:

> Nina, I think the world of her and where she has gone in her life.

Nina coped with this illness by staying positive, living every day like her last, and moving on with everyday living. She looks after her three sons and still laughs, sings, dances, and enjoys going out with friends.

This illness has made Nina a stronger person and has also enabled her to help others cope with the same illness. I believe that the sudden death of a loved one helped her cope better than she may have.

Every day I am in awe of her strength, and I will be there every step of the way in fighting this hideous battle with her.

Also a big thank-you to Richard Weinstein, photographer of the book cover. We chose a naked shot to represent that you cannot tell the scars.

A private place. There is a special rock by the ocean where I live. I call it my rock, although it really isn't just mine. I go there to watch the ocean and feel the wind and salt on my face. I sit there and stare at the world around me, and all the time I feel the courage within me growing. I smile, sigh, and reflex on my journey, while all around me is a perfect day that I can enjoy.

Laugh and laugh some more. Being positive and keeping a fun side to any battle is the way to go. Laughter is always the best medicine. In fact, laughing till you cry is great.

What makes a woman? Is it her soft skin, her tenderness, her ability to do six things at once, her patience, her love, her hair, her body? Well, it's all those things together, and more. Warmth, love, and an amazing ability to bounce back in a crisis make you a woman. Cancer is a crisis. We can bounce back stronger and better than ever. The body gets knocked around, yet it can repair itself, and that is truly amazing. Really, where are we? In reality, if you are well or sick, we may not wake tomorrow, so live every day as if it's your last. That's the secret.

I can put on a dress and high heels. I can walk past the mirror. Guess what lies beneath all of that. Reality is in the eyes of those around you. They look at me on the outside, and I know I look totally real to them. But it is on the inside where we have made all changes. Changes that give me a new me and we cheated death . . . That is amazing.

I am proud today! I will never forget *I am still a woman.*

Good journey!